BIGGEST NAMES IN SPORTS

RUSSELL WESTBROOK

BASKETBALL STAR

by Todd Kortemeier

FOCUS READERS

FOCUS READERS

WWW.FOCUSREADERS.COM

Focus Readers is distributed by North Star Editions:
sales@northstareditions.com | 888-417-0195

Produced for Focus Readers by Red Line Editorial.

Photographs ©: Nick Wass/AP Images, cover, 1; Jack Dempsey/AP Images, 4–5, 9; Michael Wyke/AP Images, 6; Paul Sakuma/AP Images, 10–11; Michael Conroy/AP Images, 13; Torrey Purvey/Icon Sportswire/AP Images, 15; Jeff Lewis/AP Images, 16–17; Julie Jacobson/AP Images, 18; Sue Ogrocki/AP Images, 21; Lucy Nicholson/AP Images, 22–23; Jeff Roberson/AP Images, 25; David J. Phillip/AP Images, 27; Red Line Editorial, 29

ISBN
978-1-63517-491-5 (hardcover)
978-1-63517-563-9 (paperback)
978-1-63517-707-7 (ebook pdf)
978-1-63517-635-3 (hosted ebook)

Library of Congress Control Number: 2017948058

Printed in the United States of America
Mankato, MN
November, 2017

ABOUT THE AUTHOR

Todd Kortemeier is a writer and editor from Minneapolis. He has authored more than 50 books for young people, primarily on sports topics. A graduate of the University of Minnesota's School of Journalism and Mass Communication, he lives in the Twin Cities with his wife.

TABLE OF CONTENTS

CHAPTER 1

The King of Triple-Doubles 5

CHAPTER 2

Hoops and Heartbreak 11

CHAPTER 3

UCLA to NBA 17

CHAPTER 4

Becoming One of the Best 23

At-a-Glance Map • 28

Focus on Russell Westbrook • 30

Glossary • 31

To Learn More • 32

Index • 32

VISIT WWW.P ENTER.COM/TOURS OR C
OKC
0
14
nuggets

CHAPTER 1

THE KING OF TRIPLE-DOUBLES

There wasn't much drama left for the Oklahoma City Thunder by the 80th game of the 2016–17 season. They had clinched a playoff spot. Even their **seed** was locked in. But their star, Russell Westbrook, had plenty to play for. He was trying to break one of the oldest records in basketball.

Westbrook takes a shot against the Denver Nuggets.

Westbrook drives toward the hoop during a 2017 game against the Houston Rockets.

Westbrook had 41 **triple-doubles** for the season. That meant in 41 games that year, he had reached double-digits in three categories such as points, **rebounds**, and **assists**. One more triple-double and he would break the

National Basketball Association (NBA) record. Hall of Famer Oscar Robertson had held the record for 55 years.

Each NBA team plays 82 games per season. The Thunder faced the Denver Nuggets in the 80th game. If Westbrook didn't break the record in this game, he would have only two more chances.

Westbrook almost broke the record in a single half. By halftime he had 23 points, 12 rebounds, and 6 assists. With four more assists in the game, he would have a triple-double.

Westbrook had three more assists in the third quarter. But by the midway point of the fourth, he was still stuck at nine.

Then with nearly four minutes to go, he spotted an open teammate. Westbrook was driving to the hoop. He saw that Semaj Christon was open behind the three-point line. Westbrook stopped his drive and dished the ball out. Christon took the shot and drained it. And just like that, Westbrook was the NBA's triple-double king.

But Westbrook wasn't done yet. The Thunder trailed by two points with only 2.9 seconds left. They needed a miracle.

Thunder center Steven Adams caught the **inbound pass**. He tossed the ball to Westbrook, who was 36 feet (11 m) from the hoop. Westbrook didn't have

Westbrook celebrates after draining the game-winning shot against the Nuggets.

time to dribble. He caught the ball and took a shot. He nailed it. Westbrook's game-winning basket gave him 50 points for the night.

It was an amazing performance. But it was just one of many in Westbrook's remarkable season.

UCLA
0

CHAPTER 2

HOOPS AND HEARTBREAK

Russell Westbrook was born in 1988. At that time, Oklahoma City could only dream of having an NBA team. But Russell did not have to dream about seeing basketball stars. Magic Johnson and the Los Angeles Lakers played just a few miles from Russell's hometown of Long Beach, California.

A young Russell Westbrook dunks the ball in a 2007 college game.

Johnson was a point guard who could do it all. He could score, pass, and rebound. Russell's father watched Johnson and the Lakers closely. Johnson became Russell's favorite player.

Soon Russell and his dad were running drills together. They worked on the same skills over and over. Russell learned how to fine-tune his shot. It was hard work. But it helped him develop the skills he needed.

In high school, Russell was the shortest player on his team. Most colleges were not interested in him. Colleges were more intrigued by his teammate, Khelcey Barrs III.

Westbrook celebrates with teammates during his first college season.

Russell stood only 5 feet 8 inches (173 cm) tall, and he weighed only 140 pounds (64 kg). But Khelcey was 6 feet 6 inches (198 cm) tall and weighed 200 pounds (91 kg). Khelcey had multiple **scholarship** offers as a 16-year-old.

Khelcey was more than Russell's teammate. The two were best friends.

They dreamed of playing together at the University of California, Los Angeles (UCLA). Sadly, that dream ended in 2004. Khelcey collapsed and died while playing in a game. He had a heart condition that nobody had known about. Russell was devastated.

REMEMBERING A FRIEND

Westbrook has never forgotten about Khelcey. The two friends always dreamed of playing in college and the NBA together. For this reason, Westbrook carries a piece of his friend with him. In every game, he wears wristbands that say "KB3." Some of his custom shoes also have Khelcey's initials and jersey number.

Westbrook wears shoes with a message that means "Rest in Peace Khelcey Barrs III."

He tried to continue the dream for both of them. He worked even harder on the court. A growth spurt helped, too. Soon he was 6 feet 3 inches (191 cm) tall and weighed 200 pounds (91 kg).

Suddenly Russell had the attention of a few colleges. He ended up choosing UCLA. His friend Khelcey was never far from his mind.

UCLA
0

CHAPTER 3

UCLA TO NBA

Other than the UCLA Bruins, there were not many college teams that wanted Russell Westbrook. However, the Bruins saw something the other teams didn't. Westbrook did not put up huge numbers. But he made the highlight reels with his dunks and athletic play.

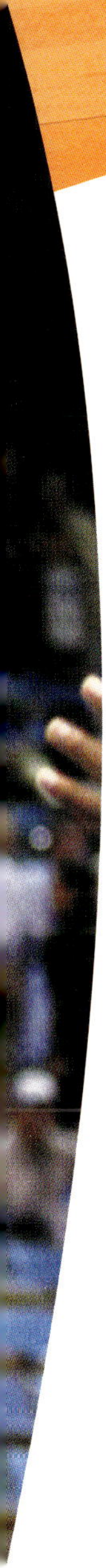

Westbrook shoots over a defender during a 2006 game against Long Beach State.

The NBA commissioner congratulates Westbrook after being drafted by the SuperSonics.

The Bruins made it to the Final Four in both of Westbrook's seasons with the team. In his second season, UCLA lost to Memphis. Many of the Memphis players said Westbrook was the toughest player on the Bruins.

In the 2008 NBA Draft, the Seattle SuperSonics took a chance. They made Westbrook the fourth overall pick. But

Westbrook never played in Seattle. The Sonics moved to Oklahoma City less than a week later. The team became known as the Thunder. Westbrook and teammate Kevin Durant led the team in its new city.

Westbrook put up an early highlight in the 2008–09 season. He hit the game-winning shot in the Thunder's first-ever win. But the Thunder won only three of their next 30 games. The young team had talent. They just had to figure out how to put it together.

The next year, the Thunder improved. They won 50 games. Westbrook and Durant dominated in a playoff win against the mighty Los Angeles Lakers.

But the Thunder lost the series in six games.

In 2010–11, Westbrook made his first All-Star Game. He put up career highs in points and assists per game. And the Thunder made it all the way to the **conference** finals. He and Durant formed one of the best partnerships in the NBA.

PLAYING FOR GOLD

Westbrook played in 28 games with the US national team from 2009 to 2012. He won a gold medal at the 2010 world championships and the 2012 Summer Olympics. Westbrook was a finalist to make the 2016 Olympic team. But he chose not to play in the tournament.

Westbrook makes a monster dunk in a 2008 game against the Memphis Grizzlies.

The duo became friends. They were both very competitive. Sometimes they argued. But they pushed each other to be better. The best was yet to come for Westbrook and the Thunder.

WEST
WEST
35

CHAPTER 4

BECOMING ONE OF THE BEST

The 2011–12 season was the Thunder's best yet. The team finally broke through to the NBA Finals. But they faced LeBron James and the Miami Heat.

The Thunder lost two of the first three games. They faced the Heat in a crucial Game 4. Russell Westbrook was brilliant.

Westbrook amazes the crowd at the 2011 All-Star Game.

He scored 43 points. Only three players since 1985 had scored more in an NBA Finals game. And 17 of his points were in the fourth quarter. When Miami went up by seven points, Westbrook scored seven in a row all by himself.

Westbrook kept his team in the game. But the Thunder found themselves down

LOOKING GOOD

One of Westbrook's biggest interests besides basketball is fashion. He has attended Fashion Week in New York City and Paris, France. In 2014, he launched his own clothing line. He also has a line of glasses. Westbrook enjoys putting together unique outfits to wear after games.

Westbrook and the Thunder came up short against the Heat in the 2012 Finals.

three points with less than 20 seconds left. Miami had the ball with five seconds on the **shot clock**. If they missed, the Thunder would get the ball back. But Westbrook chose to foul Heat player Mario Chalmers. Chalmers then hit both free throws to put the game away. The Thunder went on to lose the series.

Westbrook led the Thunder back to the playoffs the next season. But an injury forced him to miss the playoffs. He also missed nearly half of the next season.

Then at the start of the 2014–15 season, Westbrook broke his hand. He missed another 15 games. But he bounced back for a healthy 2015–16. Westbrook averaged a **double-double** for the season. And he made his first start in the All-Star Game. He was the game's most valuable player (MVP).

The 2016–17 season brought a big change. Kevin Durant left the Thunder for the Golden State Warriors. Westbrook had to lead the team all by himself. He

Westbrook competes in a 2017 playoff game against the Houston Rockets.

had his best season ever. Westbrook won the MVP award and set the record for most triple-doubles in a season. He also averaged a triple-double for the season.

One thing still eluded Westbrook. That was an NBA title. But with the way he was playing, it looked closer than ever.

RUSSELL WESTBROOK

- Height: 6 feet 3 inches (191 cm)
- Weight: 200 pounds (91 kg)
- Birth date: November 12, 1988
- Birthplace: Long Beach, California
- High school: Leuzinger High School (Lawndale, California)
- College: University of California, Los Angeles (2006–2008)
- NBA team: Oklahoma City Thunder (2008–)
- Major awards: 2012 Olympic gold medal; 2015 and 2016 All-Star Game MVP; 2015 and 2017 NBA scoring leader; 2017 NBA MVP

Los Angeles
Oklahoma City

FOCUS ON
RUSSELL WESTBROOK

Write your answers on a separate piece of paper.

1. Write a sentence that summarizes the main ideas of Chapter 2.

2. Which skill do you think is most important to Westbrook's success? Why?

3. Who was Westbrook's favorite basketball player when he was young?

   A. Magic Johnson
   B. Oscar Robertson
   C. Kevin Durant

4. Why did Westbrook foul Mario Chalmers in Game 4 of the 2012 NBA Finals?

   A. because he knew the Thunder were going to lose the game
   B. because he wanted the Heat to score more points
   C. because he hoped the Thunder would get the ball back after the free throws

Answer key on page 32.

GLOSSARY

assists

Passes that lead directly to a teammate scoring a basket.

conference

A group of teams within a league.

double-double

A game in which a player has double-digit numbers in two categories.

inbound pass

A pass made from outside the court to restart game play.

rebounds

Plays in which a player controls the ball after a missed shot.

scholarship

Money given to a student to pay for education expenses.

seed

The place a team is ranked for the playoffs.

shot clock

A timer that tracks the number of seconds until a team must shoot.

triple-doubles

Games in which a player has double-digit numbers in three categories.

TO LEARN MORE

BOOKS

Doeden, Matt. *Russell Westbrook*. Minneapolis: Lerner Publications, 2017.

Hall, Brian. *Russell Westbrook*. Minneapolis: Abdo Publishing, 2017.

Hammer, Max. *Superstars of the Oklahoma City Thunder*. Mankato, MN: Amicus, 2016.

NOTE TO EDUCATORS

Visit **www.focusreaders.com** to find lesson plans, activities, links, and other resources related to this title.

INDEX

All-Star Game, 20, 26

Barrs, Khelcey III, 12–15

Christon, Semaj, 8

Denver Nuggets, 7
Durant, Kevin, 19–20, 26

Final Four, 18

Golden State Warriors, 26

James, LeBron, 23
Johnson, Magic, 11–12

Long Beach, California, 11
Los Angeles Lakers, 11–12, 19

Miami Heat, 23–25

National Basketball Association (NBA), 7–8, 11, 14, 20, 27
NBA Draft, 18
NBA Finals, 23–24

Oklahoma City Thunder, 5, 7–8, 19–21, 23, 25–26
Olympics, 20

Robertson, Oscar, 7

Seattle SuperSonics, 18–19

University of California, Los Angeles (UCLA), 14–15, 17–18

Answer Key: 1. Answers will vary; **2.** Answers will vary; **3.** A; **4.** C